Helen Hayes

A GATHERING OF HOPE

Helen Hayes

A GATHERING OF HOPE

Phoenix Press

WALKER AND COMPANY
New York

This large print edition first published in 1984 by Walker Publishing Company, by arrangement with Fortress Press.

Printed in the United States of America

Library of Congress Cataloging in Publication Data

Main entry under title:

A Gathering of hope.

    1. Meditations.   2. Prayers.   3. Large type books.
I. Hayes, Helen, 1900-
[BV4832.2.G34 1984]   242   84-11865
ISBN 0-8027-2467-1 (lg. print)

Cover photo by Tom Gates, Pictorial Parade

Helen Hayes

A GATHERING OF HOPE

Introduction

Words take many forms. They come in countless shapes and colors. They can be coarse or elegant, gaudy or beautiful, bitter or sweet. Words have the ability to quash the soul or elevate it to heights unimaginable. They can strip you clean and leave you cold, alone, naked, worthless. But they can restore as well, being supreme company in those times of deepest need. By giving strength where there is little, words can renew a despondent soul. Further, they can illuminate a new and better path. Words can, in fact, create whole new worlds!

There is something to words, something that can, if properly employed, have mystical effects. The well-written line has a seductive power which lures a person to it. If captured, one can depart from it only for a short time before feeling the almost desperate desire to return. Conversely, months or years may pass before one rediscovers a line that had previously meant so much. Then it is the reunion of old acquaintances that fills the heart with joy.

What makes words so necessary? It may be the circumstances or the temperament of the person who encounters the words. It may be the writer's genius living on in the particular choice of sounds and syllables, meanings and implications that make up the line. Likely it is a combination of the two, each adding to the other. I have made my life one of words, and I still am not certain what is the ''tie that binds'' a person's heart so firmly to particular words. But I do know there are words to which I return again and again. I continue to feel their power. I have known and I know today their beauty. Countless times I have called upon them for comfort and inspiration. Yet, now it seems fewer and fewer people know the hopes and dreams and vital thoughts gathered into words, the portrayals of humanity—both good and bad—built into lines, the solace and strength housed in paragraphs. To counter that lack of knowledge, I offer this little book.

Here I have collected the words—the poems, the Psalms, the prayers, the lyrics, the bits of wisdom—that have stood by me and lived within me as I have pursued my career, raised my family, lived my life. They have had the ability to pull me through some of the most wonderful and some of the most tragic moments. And they are still with me today, perhaps more alive and more vibrant than when I first encountered them. They are my old and steadfast friends, friends whom I have called upon and know I may call upon again. I would like now to introduce you to, or perhaps reacquaint you with, these friends. I pray that in reading them you, too, may find the hope, the comfort, and the inspiration that have guided me through the years.

My special thanks to John Kirvan and Roger Radley for their assistance in compiling the materials in this book.

Songs of Praise

FAITH AND AFFIRMATION

I believe in God because I am an actress. As an actress I need direction. I cannot conceive of the shape of a performance without the director's hand. Similarly, I cannot conceive of the shape of my life without the divine direction of the Lord.

I enjoy acting because I listen. By listening to everyone on the set, I gain a feeling of the substance and the content of the character I'm portraying. I enjoy life for the same reason. By listening carefully to what God tells me in the voice of all things, I receive the substance and the content of my very existence. Some say that faith and religion are crutches. I am here to say that I have leaned on those crutches all the days of my life. Without them life has no meaning. Without them I could not have survived.

It's that simple. But there was a time when I was not so plain about my faith. As a Catholic married to a divorced man, I could not receive Holy Communion. Although I didn't put my religious belief entirely away, I let it rest for awhile. Things were going fairly well in my life. I was a successful actress; I had a lovely marriage and two beautiful children. Except for those unpleasant times on the road away from the family, things were fine. Then suddenly the events of my life turned and I found myself confronting the essential questions of my faith.

My daughter's illness and subsequent death was the first event that made me question why I had fallen silent in my belief for so long. After Mary died my husband, Charlie MacArthur, and I had a hard time regaining the desire to carry on. It was only the renewal of the belief I had once maintained that enabled us to see our way back to a semblance of normal life. It was then that I redis-

6

covered the beauty of the Psalms and of the Scriptures that had meant so much to me in my youth. They became our ultimate source of comfort through those hard months after Mary's death.

Then, years later, Charlie died, causing me to become even more ''public'' with my faith. Shortly after his death, I found this little line written by Richard Cecil: ''A man who puts aside his religion because he is going into society is like one taking off his shoes because he is about to walk on thorns.'' It seemed to put it all into perspective for me. I returned to the Catholic church and received instruction. However, while I didn't want to make a show of my faith, I was still more silent than I should have been.

That was twenty-five years ago. I feel freer now. I am much more free with my faith. And why not? It's a wonderful thing to know that God is present in all that we do. At times I am amazed at the form that God's inspiration and guidance takes. It never seems to come through extraordinary measures like lightning flashes or voices but instead through everyday living things. Roller-skating down the streets in Nyack with my daughter years ago was a great joy. Walking down those same streets today —remembering those wonderful times with Mary plus seeing the people of my life now who make up this little town— is equally a joy. Today is just fine.

I can never find enough words nor the proper kind of words to affirm the wonderful faith I have found. But I continue to search! Also, I carry the discipline that I learned in the theater into my faith. While I am lax about how often I read the prayer books and the Psalms, I am always sure to read them. I find a continued delight in the strength they offer me.

I am happy to profess my faith. I don't think there ever was a time in my life that I didn't feel the presence of God controlling and guiding, directing my days. That, in its simplicity, is all I can say. But that, in its greatness, is enough!

I've often felt that if I were to commission a writer, poet, philosopher, or saint to express in as few words as possible the feeling I have for life, none could do better than the words that appear here.

For all that has been,
Thanks!
For all that will be,
Yes!

Dag Hammarskjöld

Affirm the glory of God! Again and again the writers of the Old and New Testaments remind us of God's infinite power and providence. Here are but four of the many hundreds of lines that assure us of his presence.

"I am going to the Father. And I will do
    whatever you ask
for in my name, so that the Father's
    glory will be shown
through the Son."

John 14:12-13

"I am the vine, you are the branches. . . .
    If you remain in
me, and my words remain in you, then
    you will ask for
anything you wish, and you shall have
    it."

John 15:5, 7

''The Father will give you anything you
    ask of him in my
name. . . .Ask and you will receive, so
    that your happiness
may be complete.''

John 16:23b, 24b

''And so I say to you: Ask, and you will
    receive; seek, and you
will find; knock, and the door will be
    opened to you. For
everyone who asks will receive, and he
    who seeks will find,
and the door will be opened to him who
    knocks.''

Luke 11:9-10

There was a period in my life when all things—career, family, home—were going well. Then Mary became ill and eventually died. It took a long time for Charlie and me to adjust to her absence. But one day, sitting by the pool at our home on the Hudson, I found this:

Late have I loved you,
O Beauty so ancient and so new;
late have I loved you!
For behold you were within me,
and I outside;
and I sought you outside
and in my unloveliness
fell upon those lovely things
that you have made.
You were with me
and I was not with you.
I was kept from you by those things,
yet had they not been in you
they would not have been at all.

You did call and cry to me
and break open my deafness;
and you sent forth your beams
to shine upon me
and chase away my blindness.
You breathed fragrance upon me,
and I drew in my breath
and do now pant for you;
I tasted you
and now hunger and thirst for you.
You touched me,
and I burned for your peace.

St. Augustine

At St. Anne's, the little church to which I belong in Nyack, they are quite fond of singing modern songs. I think they are lovely, and of them this is one of my favorites. Perhaps we should all be willing to sing songs to God like "Annie's Song," which is, after all, a hymn of praise!

Annie's Song

You fill up my senses like a night in a
    forest
Like the mountains in Springtime, like a
    walk in the rain.
Like a storm in the desert, like a sleepy
    blue ocean
You fill up my senses, come fill me
    again.

Come let me love you, let me give my
    life to you
Let me drown in your laughter, let me
    die in your arms.
Let me lay down beside you, let me
    always be with you
Come let me love you, come love me
    again.

John Denver

There is another modern hymn that we sing at St. Anne's. It begins with these words: "I believe in the sun even when it isn't shining." I wouldn't be surprised if it is based on this poem by Emily Dickinson.

I never saw a Moor—
I never saw the Sea—
Yet know I how the Heather looks
And what a wave must be.

I never spoke with God
Nor visited in Heaven—
Yet certain am I of the spot
As if the chart were given—

Emily Dickinson

Let nothing disturb you,
let nothing frighten you,
all things are passing;
God only is changeless.
Patience gains all things.
Who has God wants nothing—
God alone fulfills.

St. Teresa of Avila

I was first taken by this poem because I love to stitch. I've always a needle and thread with which I am mending things and making them right again. I spied Taylor's poem one day just after I had put my sewing down, and it has been with me since.

Housewifery

Make me, O Lord, thy spinning wheel
    complete.
Thy holy word my distaff make for me.
Make mine affections thy swift flyers
    neat;
And make my soul thy holy spool to be.
My conversation make to be thy reel,
And reel the yarn thereon spun of thy
    wheel.

Make me thy loom then, knit therein
    this twine;
And make thy Holy Spirit, Lord, wind
    quills.

Then weave the web thyself. The yarn
  is fine.
Thine ordinances make my fulling mills.
Then dye the same in heavenly colors
  choice,
All pinked with varnished flowers of
  paradise.

Then clothe therewith mine
  understanding, will
Affections, judgment, conscience,
  memory
My words and actions, that their shine
  may fill
My ways with glory and thee glorify.
Then mine apparel shall display before
  ye
That I am clothed in holy robes for
  glory.

Edward Taylor

Devotion

The heart can think of no devotion
Greater than being shore to the ocean—
Holding the curve of one position,
Counting an endless repetition.

Robert Frost

Here are three Psalms followed by three poems that for me sing praise to the Lord. They are simple in their message. I think they speak for themselves.

❖

O come, let us sing unto the Lord: let us
    make a joyful
noise to the rock of our salvation.

Let us come before his presence with
    thanksgiving, and make
a joyful noise unto him with psalms.

For the Lord is a great God, and a great
    King above all gods.

In his hand are the deep places of the
    earth: the strength
of the hills is his also.

The sea is his, and he made it: and his
    hands formed the
dry land.

O come, let us worship and bow down:
    let us kneel before
the Lord our maker.

For he is our God: and we are the
    people of his pasture, and
the sheep of his hand.

Psalm 95:1-7

Lord, thou hast been our dwelling place
    in all generations.

Before the mountains were brought
    forth, or ever thou hadst
formed the earth and the world, even
    from everlasting to
everlasting, thou art God.

Thou turnest man to destruction; and
    sayest, Return, ye
children of men.

For a thousand years in thy sight are
    but as yesterday when
it is past, and as a watch in the night.

Thou carriest them away as with a
    flood; they are as a sleep:
in the morning they are like grass which
    groweth up.

In the morning it flourisheth, and
    groweth up; in the evening
it is cut down, and withereth. . . .

O satisfy us early with thy mercy; that
    we may rejoice and
be glad all our days.

Make us glad according to the days
	wherein thou hast
afflicted us, and the years wherein we
	have seen evil.

Let thy work appear unto thy servants,
	and thy glory unto
their children.

And let the beauty of the Lord our God
	be upon us: and
establish thou the work of our hands
	upon us: yea, the work
of our hands establish thou it.

Psalm 90:1-6, 14-17

✣

In thee, O Lord, do I put my trust: let
    me never be put to
confusion.

Deliver me in thy righteousness, and
    cause me to escape:
incline thine ear unto me, and save me.

Be thou my strong habitation,
    whereunto I may continually
resort: thou hast given commandment
    to save me; for
thou art my rock and my fortress.

Deliver me, O my God, out of the hand
    of the wicked, out of
the hand of the unrighteous and cruel
    man.

For thou art my hope, O Lord God: thou
    art my trust from
my youth.

By thee have I been holden up from the
    womb: thou art he
that took me out of my mother's
    bowels: my praise shall
be continually of thee.

I am as a wonder unto many; but thou
art my strong refuge.

Let my mouth be filled with thy praise
and with thy honour
all the day.

Cast me not off in the time of old age;
forsake me not when
my strength faileth.

Psalm 71:1-9

It is not growing like a tree
In bulk, doth make man better be;
Or standing long an oak, three hundred
    year,
To fall a log, at last, dry, bald, and sere:
A lily of a day
Is fairer far in May,
Although it fall, and die that night;
It was the plant and flower of light.
In small proportions we just beauties
    see:
And in short measures, life may perfect
    be.

Ben Jonson

✿

When in disgrace with Fortune and
     men's eyes
I all alone beweep my outcast state,
And trouble deaf heaven with my
     bootless cries,
And look upon myself and curse my
     fate,
Wishing me like to one more rich in
     hope,
Featur'd like him, like him with friends
     possess'd,
Desiring this man's art, and that man's
     scope,
With what I most enjoy contented
     least;
Yet in these thoughts myself almost
     despising,

Haply I think on thee, and then my
      state,
(Like to the lark at break of day arising
From sullen earth) sings hymns at
      heaven's gate,
    For thy sweet love rememb'red such
      wealth brings,
    That then I scorn to change my state
      with kings.

          William Shakespeare

A Song to David

He sang of God—the mighty source
Of all things—the stupendous force
On which all strength depends;
From whose right arm, beneath whose
    eyes,
All period, power, and enterprize
Commences, reigns, and ends. . . .

The world—the clustering spheres he
    made,
The glorious light, the soothing shade,
Dale, champaign, grove, and hill;
The multitudinous abyss,
Where Secrecy remains in bliss,
And Wisdom hides her skill. . . .

"Tell them I am," Jehova said
To Moses; while earth heard in dread,
And smitten to the heart
At once above, beneath, around,
All nature, without voice or sound,
Replied, "O Lord, Thou art."

                Christopher Smart

To Be Born
Is to Live and to Die

YOUTH, AGE,
AND THE CERTAINTY OF DEATH

I am old now and I'm going to die. And yet, I am living in a time that puts a premium on youth, a time so self-conscious about becoming old and dying that it will not even allow use of the proper words. We have all sorts of euphemisms for aging: the sunset years, the autumn of one's life, the golden years. When it comes to the real issue, there are more: he passed away; she has left for the eternal spring; they've joined the blessed flock. But these are simply cushions to pad the soul from the more crushing word: death. The word is death. For me it's most simple. I am old now and I'm going to die.

Life for me has been a constant and recurrent celebration of my usefulness. On the stage, in my home, with my family and friends, I have gained the most joy from the thought that I have helped, served, mended in some good way. For me the act of living, of looking ahead, has meant to hope that my words and actions will make someone's life a little richer.

But, to paraphrase the Bible, where is the sting in the fact that I will someday die? Rather, I would tend to agree with Thomas Jefferson, who once said, "My only fear is that I may live too long." When I think about getting older, I wish and pray that I will not live life beyond my usefulness in this world. That I won't live so long that dying has no significance to me. That I won't live beyond the point of caring.

When I was younger and on the road a great deal, we had a nurse to care for the children when I was away. She is ninety-seven now and lives in a nursing home because she is unable to care for herself. She doesn't look forward to anything. Furthermore, she has reached the point where she doesn't have any hope, even in death. I am sad to think that such a thing can happen, for to lose all hope is not to live. Hope is all we really know. When it ceases life and the future cease with it.

The very thought of hopelessness frightens me because I have been so close to that miserable state myself in the past. My daughter died when she was very young, and for a long, long while it was a struggle for me to accept death happening to someone as young and as beautiful as she. It was even more of a struggle continuing to live in those months and years that followed. But we managed together, the family and I, with not a little help from the comfort offered by the words that follow. I learned that Mary didn't die in vain. Short as her life was—just nineteen years—it made a mark on the world. She was a lovely person and great to live with.

Years later I was forced face-to-face with death again. Though I had experi-

33

enced the emotions and tragedy of losing a dear person before, Charlie's death was not an easy cross to bear. Again I turned desperately, though confidently, to the solace and promise offered in poems, prayers, and the Psalms. I guess I am protected by my desire for happiness. As long as there is a smidgen, a crumb, of happiness to be grasped in life, I will grasp for it.

I've always been amazed and somewhat amused to view how people's struggles change as they grow older. It seems to me that the source of trouble wells from entirely different springs for the young than for the old. I am old now, and so I think much more about death than I do about love. It is with a marked irony and perhaps a little elitism of age that I view and, indeed, remember the agonies of youth.

As so many others, I was an unrequited lover! There was hardly a time in my early theater career that I did not spend tortured in secret love for some young man who was playing the same stage as I. It was all such a self-conscious part of my life. It's odd. I was more concerned with the way I looked and acted backstage and during rehearsals to the man of my heart's fancy than I was about my presence on the stage before thousands of critical eyes each night! And, like every other person in love for the first or fiftieth time, how I suffered, that is, until the next ''object of obscure desire'' came along!

But my early career was also a time of soul-searching. In times of need I relied on the power found in great words. I read the Bible and recited the Psalms, which I had been raised to do. Also, reciting the sonnets of Shakespeare became a glorious habit after a very wise acting coach ordered me to read them aloud to improve my accent.

During those years I fell deeply in love with and eventually married Charlie Mac-Arthur, a journalist and playwright. Both Charlie and our circle of literary and theater friends kept me constantly under the influence of fine words. To those words I have always turned, searching them in my times of greatest need: in death and in love and in the act of living from one day to the next.

Below appear but a few of the writings that have given me the resilience to outlast the heartbreak of outrageous loves and the oppressive imminence of my own death and the deaths of those close to me. These writings are among the oldest, most beloved, items in my ''repertoire.'' They have been with me from my youth. They have withstood the test of time.

To grow old is to watch many good people die: loved ones, dear friends, people you don't even know. In the face of it all we must believe, as Donne believed, that we will all awake eternally and that death will be no more.

❧

Death, be not proud, though some have
    called thee
Mighty and dreadful, for thou art not so;
For those whom thou think'st thou dost
    overthrow
Die not, poor Death, nor yet canst thou
    kill me.
From rest and sleep, which but thy
    pictures be,
Much pleasure; then from thee much
    more must flow,
And soonest our best men with thee do
    go,
Rest of their bones, and soul's delivery.
Thou art slave to fate, chance, kings,
    and desperate men,
And dost with poison, war, and
    sickness dwell,

And poppy or charms can make us
sleep as well
And better than thy stroke; why
swell'st thou then?
One short sleep past, we wake
eternally
And death shall be no more; Death,
thou shalt die.

John Donne

With age comes the tendency to summon up the people, places, and events of days gone by. But that tendency is far from being melancholy. Thoughts of good times spent, combined with the hope of a new life in the future, are very joyous!

When to the sessions of sweet silent
    thought
I summon up remembrance of things
    past,
I sigh the lack of many a thing I sought,
And with old woes new wail my dear
    time's waste;
Then can I drown an eye (unus'd to
    flow)
For precious friends hid in death's
    dateless night,
And weep afresh love's long since
    cancell'd woe,
And moan th' expense of many a
    vanish'd sight;
Then can I grieve at grievances
    foregone,

And heavily from woe to woe tell o'er
The sad account of fore-bemoaned
    moan,
Which I new pay as if not paid before:
  But if the while I think on thee, dear
    friend,
  All losses are restor'd, and sorrows
    end.

                William Shakespeare

When I first found Emily Dickinson's poem, I was startled. It was so true to my own experience that I was sure she must have written it about me. I lost two very dear people, and so have often felt that "my life closed twice."

❧

My life closed twice before its close—
It yet remains to see
If Immortality unveil
A third event to me

So huge, so hopeless to conceive
As these that twice befell.
Parting is all we know of heaven,
And all we need of hell.

Emily Dickinson

When passionate love is abruptly called short, the results can be devastating. But though it never seemed so at the time, I soon learned that which Tennyson held is true:

'Tis better to have loved and lost
Than never to have loved at all.

Alfred Lord Tennyson

I am so frequently asked which was my most memorable performance. There have been many important and meaningful moments in my career and it is hard to isolate one from the others. But I think the most passionate performances I have given have been to no one but myself—or perhaps to a few close friends. It is at those times that I can entirely let myself go and forget the proper methods of stage performance. I allow myself to become emotionally and physically involved with the role.

I have long felt Hecuba's lament to the Greeks for the murder of her son after the fall of Troy to be one of the most lucid and vibrant speeches in the history of the theater. Once, while touring Greece with friends, I visited Epidaurus. There, in the ancient theater built for nearly fifteen-thousand people, I took the stage and, to an audience of two, delivered Hecuba's lines from **The Trojan Women.**

Set the shield down—the great round
    shield of Hector.
I wish I need not look at it.
You Greeks, your spears are sharp but
    not your wits.
You feared a child. You murdered him.
Strong murder. You were frightened,
    then? You thought
he might build up our ruined Troy? And
    yet
when Hector fought and thousands at
    his side,
we fell beneath you. Now, when all is
    lost,
the city captured and the Trojans dead,
a little child like this made you afraid.
The fear that comes when reason goes
    away—
Myself, I do not wish to share it.
Beloved, what a death has come to
    you.
If you had fallen fighting for the city,
If you had known strong youth and love
and godlike power, if we could think
you had known happiness—if there is

happiness anywhere—
But now—you saw and knew, but with
your soul
you did not know, and what was in
your house
you could not use.
Poor little one. How savagely our
ancient walls,
Apollo's towers, have torn away the
curls
your mother's fingers wound and where
she pressed
her kisses—here where the broken
bone grins white—
Oh no—I cannot—
Dear hands, the same dear shape your
father's had,
how loosely now you fall. And dear
proud lips
forever closed. False words you spoke
to me
when you would jump into my bed, call
me sweet names
and tell me, Grandmother, when you
are dead,
I'll cut off a great lock of hair and lead
my soldiers all

to ride out past your tomb.
Not you, but I, old, homeless, childless,
must lay you in your grave, so young,
so miserably dead.
Dear God. How you would run to greet
    me.
And I would nurse you in my arms, and
    oh,
so sweet to watch you sleep. All gone.
What could a poet carve upon your
    tomb?
"A child lies here whom the Greeks
    feared and slew."
Ah, Greece should boast of that.
Child, they have taken all that was your
    father's,
but one thing, for your burying, you
    shall have,
the bronze-barred shield.
It kept safe Hector's mighty arm, but
    now
it has lost its master.
The grip of his own hand has marked it
    —dear to me then—
His sweat has stained the rim. Often
    and often

in battle it rolled down from brows and
    beard
while Hector held the shield close.
Come, bring such covering for the pitiful
    dead body
as we still have. God has not left us
    much
to make a show with. Everything I have
I give you, child.
O men, secure when once good fortune
    comes—
fools, fools. Fortune's ways—
here now, there now. She springs
away—back—and away, an idiot's
    dance.
No one is ever always fortunate.

                   Euripides

The following two poems show how, in the face of all adversity, we tenaciously hang on to love.

Reluctance

Out through the fields and the woods
   And over the walls I have wended;
I have climbed the hills of view
   And looked at the world, and
     descended;
I have come by the highway home,
   And lo, it is ended.

The leaves are all dead on the ground,
   Save those that the oak is keeping
To ravel them one by one
   And let them go scraping and
     creeping
Out over the crusted snow,
   When others are sleeping.

And the dead leaves lie huddled and
     still,
   No longer blown hither and thither;
The last lone aster is gone;

The flowers of the witch-hazel wither;
The heart is still aching to seek,
  But the feet question "Whither?"

Ah, when to the heart of man
  Was it ever less than a treason
To go with the drift of things,
  To yield with a grace to reason,
And bow and accept the end
  Of a love or a season?

                              Robert Frost

Love is not all: it is not meat nor drink
Nor slumber nor a roof against the rain;
Nor yet a floating spar to men that sink
And rise and sink and rise and sink
again;
Love can not fill the thickened lung with
breath,
Nor clean the blood, nor set the
fractured bone;
Yet many a man is making friends with
death
Even as I speak, for lack of love alone.
It well may be that in a difficult hour,
Pinned down by pain and moaning for
release,
Or nagged by want past resolution's
power,
I might be driven to sell your love for
peace,
Or trade the memory of this night for
food.
It well may be. I do not think I would.

          Edna St. Vincent Millay

Charlie introduced me to this poem shortly after we met. We often took the ferries and the train north for no reason but to be alone with one another. One day, on the ferry across the Hudson, Charlie showed me this:

Recuerdo

We were very tired, we were very
    merry—
We had gone back and forth all night on
    the ferry.
It was bare and bright, and smelled like
    a stable—
But we looked into a fire, we leaned
    across a table,
We lay on a hill-top underneath the
    moon;
And the whistles kept blowing, and the
    dawn came soon.

We were very tired, we were very
    merry—
We had gone back and forth all night on
    the ferry;

And you ate an apple, and I ate a pear,
From a dozen of each we had bought
      somewhere;
And the sky went wan, and the wind
      came cold,
And the sun rose dripping, a bucketful
      of gold.

We were very tired, we were very
      merry,
We had gone back and forth all night on
      the ferry.
We hailed, "Good morrow, mother!" to
      a shawl-covered head,
And bought a morning paper, which
      neither of us read;
And she wept, "God bless you!" for
      the apples and pears,
And we gave her all our money but our
      subway fares.

                    Edna St. Vincent Millay

❦

Wherefore should I fear in the days of
        evil, when the iniquity
of my heels shall compass me about?

They that trust in their wealth, and
        boast themselves in the
multitude of their riches;

None of them can by any means
        redeem his brother, nor give
to God a ransom for him:

(For the redemption of their soul is
        precious, and it ceaseth
for ever:)

That he should still live for ever, and
        not see corruption.

For he seeth that wise men die,
        likewise the fool and the
brutish person perish, and leave their
        wealth to others.

Their inward thought is, that their
        houses shall continue for
ever, and their dwelling places to all
        generations; they call
their lands after their own names.

Nevertheless man being in honour
        abideth not: he is like the
beasts that perish.

This their way is their folly: yet their
        posterity approve their
sayings. Selah.

Like sheep they are laid in the grave;
        death shall feed on
them; and the upright shall have
        dominion over them in the
morning; and their beauty shall
        consume in the grave from
their dwelling.

But God will redeem my soul from the
        power of the grave:
for he shall receive me. Selah.

Be not thou afraid when one is made
        rich, when the glory of
his house is increased;

For when he dieth he shall carry nothing
        away: his glory shall
not descend after him.

Though while he lived he blessed his
        soul, And men will

praise thee, when thou doest well to
    thyself.

He shall go to the generation of his
    fathers; they shall never
see light.

Man that is in honour, and
    understandeth not, is like the
beasts that perish.

Psalm 49

Ode to Life

Life! I know not what thou art,
But know that thou and I must part;
And when, or how, or where we met,
I own to me's a secret yet.

  Life! we've been long together
Through pleasant and through cloudy
      weather;
'Tis hard to part when friends are
      dear,—
Perhaps 'twill cost a sigh, a tear;
—Then steal away, give little warning,
  Choose thine own time,
Say not Good Night,—but in some
      brighter clime
  Bid me Good Morning.

Anna Letitia Barbauld

I will never read this without thinking first of Mary and then of Charles. If my love could have saved them, they never would have died.

In Memory of Those Loved

May you always walk in sunshine
and God's love around you flow;
For the happiness you gave us,
No one will ever know.
It broke our hearts to lose you,
But you did not go alone;
A part of us went with you
The day God called you home.
A million times we've needed you,
A million times we've cried.
If love could only have saved you,
You never would have died.

Traditional Irish

A Gathering of Hope

HOPE AND FEAR

After the earth was formed, says the Greek creation myth, the gods delegated the creation of man to the wise Titan Prometheus and to his scatterbrained brother, Epimetheus. Prometheus fashioned man out of mud, then gave Epimetheus the task of parceling out varied characteristics to man and animals in order to distinguish one from the other.

Without much forethought Epimetheus set about his task, giving this creature speed and that creature stealth, this one claws and that one teeth, and so on, until he came to man. He then realized that he had nothing left to give. Upon discovering what his brother had done, Prometheus went to the sun and lit a torch, delivering fire to mankind.

Zeus and the other gods were angered by this gift of fire. They were also angry at Prometheus for other ways that he helped man. So they pondered a way to punish mankind for accepting Prometheus's gifts. Finally, they consorted to create woman, each god contributing something to make her most beautiful. Naming her Pandora, they sent her to earth where she became Epimetheus's wife, much to the warning of Prometheus.

One day, in the home of Epimetheus, Pandora discovered a sealed jar in which Epimetheus had stored every sort of noxious thing that he had found unworthy to assign to creation. Being made with the gift of curiosity, Pandora unsealed the jar, letting loose all the plagues and molestations known to mankind. She tried in vain to reseal the jar, but it was too late. All within had escaped—except for one thing. Peering into the bottom of the jar, she spied one great virtue that Epimetheus had mistakenly placed into the vile jar: hope. Thus, while humanity faces many evils in the world, it still possesses hope.

I resent the so-called modern poets, philosophers, and authors who seek to strip humanity of all hope. Those gifted and persuasive talents paint such a bleak and nihilistic picture of humanity. To listen to those dark prognosticators and to adhere to their tenets is to give up even the very thought of hope. If they had their way, hope might remain sealed in Epimetheus's jar—away from humanity—to this day!

It is fashionable to speak and write of this life as an end in itself, of there being nothing beyond that which is here and now. It is fashionable to ask the great questions—Is there a God? Is there more?—and then go to the grave protesting that no answer has come. But it is the very characteristic of hope that makes us what we are. Our innate capacity to see beyond our present existence to something future, something perhaps better, is what makes humanity so glorious. To cut ourselves off from that is to amputate a vital and necessary part. And for what end?

I remember with what joy I read the final pages of **Grendel,** a little book written by John Gardner. Before that point in my reading I had been discouraged, thinking the book another in a tradition of cynical betrayals of all that is wonderful in humanity. Throughout the book Grendel, the hated beast of the Beowulf epic, is allowed to speak. He treats his foe, humanity, so critically and nastily! And with what sheer satisfaction does he set about to kill and consume its members! Were it not for the brevity of the book, I'm sure I would have abandoned it. But I kept with it, and in the end the hero, Beowulf, prevails—gloriously!! In the splendidly written final pages, Beowulf defeats not only the bleak, cynical beast but also the attitudes it holds. While up until the last the beast is so smug and so powerful that it appears all hope is lost, in the end humanity wins out—gloriously, heroically, confidently. Hope is restored; that which makes us human has emerged intact from perilous odds.

There are times when life's events strip away all hope. Those moments, when there is nothing ahead and nothing behind, are the darkest and bleakest times for the soul. They're times of desperation. Having been emotionally and bodily drained, a person has no strength to proceed.

I have known those times: the death of my Mary, Charlie's absence during the war, the death of my mother, those occasions when it seemed like I'd been on the road playing before the eyes of people for too long. I suppose I lost hope then. But I never lost **all** hope. There is a vast difference. To lose all hope is to lose the hope of God, of faith. It is to lose hope in the power of glorious words, those tools of the Lord with which he mends us and puts us on our way. It is to live a life in constant fear, fear of things both seen and unseen.

In those times when fears and bleak miseries have crowded into my life, in those times of sickness and loss when I thought I might not last the terrible "slings and arrows of outrageous fortune," I have sought out, sometimes desperately, sometimes despondently, the following words. They have always restored my hope and calmed my fear. And allowed me to carry on.

The night the American troops landed in Normandy, I knew Charlie would be there. Anxious and unable to sleep, I took my book of Psalms and searched for the Ninety-third. Somehow my glance fell on this instead, the fortieth. The idea of God inclining unto me has been from that night on a constant source of comfort.

✤

I waited patiently for the Lord; and he
        inclined unto me, and
heard my cry.

He brought me up also out of an
        horrible pit, out of the
miry clay, and set my feet upon a rock,
        and established my
goings.

And he hath put a new song in my
        mouth, even praise unto
our God: many shall see it, and fear,
        and shall trust in the
Lord.

Blessed is that man that maketh the
      Lord his trust, and
respecteth not the proud, nor such as
      turn aside to lies.

Many, O Lord my God, are thy
      wonderful works which thou
hast done, and thy thoughts which are
      to us-ward: they
cannot be reckoned up in order unto
      thee: if I would declare
and speak of them, they are more than
      can be numbered. . . .

Let all those that seek thee rejoice and
      be glad in thee: let
such as love thy salvation say
      continually, The Lord be
magnified.

Psalm 40:1-5, 16

Sometimes the simplest statement, direct and terse, has the most effect on the soul. With a command the Lord tells us, his children, to behave!

"Be still, and know that I am God."

Psalm 46:10

Here are other favorites:

To travel hopefully is a better thing than
    to arrive.

        Robert Louis Stevenson

Work without Hope draws nectar in a
    sieve,
And Hope without an object cannot
    live.

        S. T. Coleridge

The prophet of despair gains a shouting
    audience. But
one who speaks from hope will be
    heard long
after the noise has died down.

                John La Farge

❖

O Lord, be not far from me;
O my help, hasten to aid me.

                Psalm 22:20

✣

And I saw a new heaven and a new
earth: for the first
heaven and the first earth were passed
away; and there was
no more sea. And I John saw the holy
city, new Jerusalem,
coming down from God out of heaven,
prepared as a bride
adorned for her husband. And I heard a
great voice out of
heaven saying, Behold, the tabernacle
of God is with men,
and he will dwell with them, and they
shall be his people, and
God himself shall be with them, and be
their God. And God
shall wipe away all tears from their
eyes; and there shall be
no more death, neither sorrow, nor
crying, neither shall there
be any more pain: for the former things
are passed away.

Revelation 21:1-4

The Night Is Not Dark

They tell of Adam:

How frightened he must have been
      when,
for the first time, he saw the sun
      disappear,
ending the light of day.

It was Adam's first darkness.

How could he accept the night, when
      he had
never seen a dawn?

After the splendor of the sun, how dark
      the darkness
was for him; how desperate the long
      terror of
the first fall of night . . . until Adam
      learned that day would
come again; could see that there is light
      and order
in the universe.

And then Adam began to see how
      much light remains
in the sky at night: the stars,
and their enduring promise of the sun,

the returning star of day.

Adam learned that the night is never
    wholly dark,
and that no night is endless.

Even as each of us must learn it,
in our own times of trouble and
    darkness.

The light is never far.

            Victor Ratner and Rabbi Bernard
                        Mandelbaum

I shall know why—when Time is over—
And I have ceased to wonder why—
Christ will explain each separate
     anguish
In the fair schoolroom of the sky—

He will tell me what "Peter" promised—
And I—for wonder at his woe—
I shall forget the drop of Anguish
That scalds me now—that scalds me
     now!

Emily Dickinson

When I Have Fears

When I have fears that I may cease to
   be
  Before my pen has glean'd my
   teeming brain,
Before high-piled books, in charact'ry,
  Hold like rich garners the full-ripen'd
   grain;
When I behold, upon the night's starr'd
   face,
  Huge cloudy symbols of a high
   romance,
And think that I may never live to trace
  Their shadows, with the magic hand
   of chance;
And when I feel, fair creature of an
   hour,
  That I shall never look upon thee
   more,

Never have relish in the faery power
   Of unreflecting love!—then on the
     shore
Of the wide world I stand alone, and
     think
Till Love and Fame to nothingness do
     sink.

                 John Keats

"Hope" is the thing with feathers—
That perches in the soul—
And sings the tune without the
    words—
And never stops—at all—

And sweetest—in the Gale—is
    heard—
And sore must be the storm—
That could abash the little Bird
That kept so many warm—

I've heard it in the chillest land—
And on the strangest Sea—
Yet, never, in Extremity,
It asked a crumb—of Me.

Emily Dickinson

The Waking

I wake to sleep, and take my waking
  slow.
I feel my fate in what I cannot fear.
I learn by going where I have to go.

We think by feeling. What is there to
  know?
I hear my being dance from ear to ear.
I wake to sleep, and take my waking
  slow.

Of those so close beside me, which are
  you?
God bless the Ground! I shall walk
  softly there,
And learn by going where I have to go.

Light takes the Tree; but who can tell
  us how?
The lowly worm climbs up a winding
  stair;
I wake to sleep, and take my waking
  slow.

Great Nature has another thing to do
To you and me; so take the lively air,

And, lovely, learn by going where to
    go.

This shaking keeps me steady. I should
    know.
What falls away is always. And is near.
I wake to sleep, and take my waking
    slow.
I learn by going where I have to go.

Theodore Roethke

Things That Never Die

The pure, the bright, the beautiful
   That stirred our hearts in youth,
The impulses to wordless prayer,
   The streams of love and truth;
The longings after something lost,
   The spirit's yearning cry,
The striving after better hopes—
   These things can never die.

Author Unknown

Credo

I cannot find my way: there is no star
In all the shrouded heavens anywhere;
And there is not a whisper in the air
Of any living voice but one so far
That I can hear it only as a bar
Of lost, imperial music, played when
    fair
And angel fingers wove, and unaware,
Dead leaves to garlands where no roses
    are.

No, there is not a glimmer, nor a call,
For one that welcomes, welcomes
    when he fears,
The black and awful chaos of the night;
For through it all—above, beyond it
    all—
I know the far-sent message of the
    years,
I feel the coming glory of the Light.

           Edwin Arlington Robinson

God is our refuge and strength, a very
present help in
trouble.

Therefore will not we fear, though the
earth be removed,
and though the mountains be carried
into the midst of the sea;

Though the waters thereof roar and be
troubled, though
the mountains shake with the swelling
thereof. Selah.

There is a river, the streams whereof
shall make glad the
city of God, the holy place of the
tabernacles of the Most
High.

God is in the midst of her; she shall not
be moved: God
shall help her, and that right early.

Psalm 46:1-5

Hear my cry, O God; attend unto my
    prayer.

From the end of the earth will I cry unto
        thee, when my
heart is overwhelmed: lead me to the
        rock that is higher
than I.

For thou hast been a shelter for me, and
        a strong tower
from the enemy.

Psalm 61:1-3

One Before Many

FAME AND LONELINESS

I suppose to some I am a "famous" person. I do appreciate being appreciated. But I have never been able to understand exactly what being a famous person means, nor in the past have I been able to handle such an attribution well. I simply have an occupation that puts me in front of the public a great deal. I have always hoped that through my performances and my words I have given some slight thing to my audience: a new perspective, an answer to a question, or perhaps even a chance to escape for a moment into my characters. If I have achieved this, and if for this I have gained fame, then I am happy enough.

But what is fame after the seeming love and adulation of the masses is subtracted? The remainder has sometimes been a source of great distress to me.

To maintain fame as an actress, one must perform in many places. One of the hardest things has always been traveling on the road, away from my home on the Hudson. It was especially bad during those years when I had Charlie and my children waiting there for my tour to end. I spent some of the loneliest times in alien hotel and boarding rooms. But to practice my art, or simply to earn bread for the table as an actress, means many, many months on the road.

It seems the more acclaimed you are in this popular business, the lonelier the situation can become. Often on the road I was forced to remain either guarded or escorted. Sequestered altogether from the outside world, I would remain either in my room or the theater. Too many people who, ostensibly, loved me would recognize me if I were to roam about in public! Since that major source of dis-traction was unavailable to me, the boredom and the loneliness were great. All I had to help me through these times, vacant except for the eight perfor-mances per week, were the blessed readings which I always had at my side. There is an expression—and I don't know where it originated—that "it's lonely at the top." Although I can safely say that I was never "at the top," I can also say that with fame came some of the loneliest times I have known.

With age and with the inspiration of my cherished words, I have overcome loneliness. I now ignore it. In fact, I don't just ignore it; I deny it! I deny that it's a necessary state of being. There's so much around me. My only trouble now is trying to find enough time for solitude, which I crave. I think it's very important to be alone. Loneliness is just an idea that, I'm afraid, has something to do with self-pity.

There is another aspect to this "fame" thing which to this day constantly affects me. It's the responsibility that comes with fame. People look up to you. Though it may be wrong, inevitably there will be those who idolize and hang on your every movement. Therefore, for humanity's sake, I have always wished to do the best I could do in my actions and in my performances. I still to this day turn down, out of conscience, a good many more roles than I play. And don't think that the money isn't needed! But I simply cannot allow myself to participate in things that I feel are destructive to the human spirit.

On the other side of the coin, I delight in roles that allow me to affirm the goodness of humanity. Every day I try to carry a vision of God's will into my activities. How can I serve? Your will, not mine, be done. These thoughts go everywhere with me. They help me exercise my willpower without getting into too much trouble. With them as guides, I feel I am doing the Master's work in the same way that a disciple or missionary might. In many ways I have the ability to reach more people than the ordinary missionary can. The people have given me this ability through their support of what I do. As long as I am able to please the people, I will continue.

On the occasion of a theater opening, Samuel Johnson once wrote the following on a playbill's cover: ''The drama's laws, the drama's patrons give. For we that live to please, must please to live.'' I think that is a wonderful way to put it. There it is, the people's responsibility to the actor and the actor's responsibility to the audience. When I'm reviewing scripts sent to me for consideration, rarely a day goes by that I don't muse on those words.

Here are other words, read and embraced when I have been alone and far from home. They are some of the words I have adopted as guidelines by which I properly exercise my fame. I hope there is a light or two to illuminate your dark times as well.

O, never say that I was false of heart,
Though absence seem'd my flame to
    qualify;
As easy might I from myself depart
As from my soul which in thy breast
    doth lie:
That is my home of love; if I have
    rang'd,
Like him that travels I return again,
Just to the time, not with the time
    exchang'd,
So that myself bring water for my stain.
Never believe, though in my nature
    reign'd
All frailties that besiege all kinds of
    blood,
That it could so preposterously be
    stain'd
To leave for nothing all thy sum of
    good;
  For nothing this wide universe I call,
  Save thou, my rose, in it thou art my
    all.

William Shakespeare

If I am successful in this, if I can reach just a few people with this message through my work on the stage, then my life has been complete.

✣

Lord, make me an instrument of your
        peace.
Where there is hatred, let me sow love;
where there is injury, pardon;
where there is doubt, faith;
where there is despair, hope;
where there is darkness, light;
where there is sadness, joy.
O Divine Master,
grant that I may not so much seek
to be consoled as to console,
to be understood as to understand,
to be loved as to love.
For it is in giving that we receive;
it is in pardoning that we are pardoned;
and it is in dying
that we are born to eternal life.

St. Francis of Assisi

As an actress I have consistently been reminded of my orientation to all human-ity. And in those times when I long to abandon it all, Donne brings me back.

⚜

No man is an island, entire of itself;
    every man is a piece of
the continent, a part of the main. If a
    clod be washed away
by the sea, Europe is the less, as well
    as if a promontory
were, as well as if a manor of thy
    friend's or of thine own
were. Any man's death diminishes me
    because I am involved
in mankind. And therefore never send
    to know for whom the
bell tolls; it tolls for thee.

John Donne

Lead, Kindly Light

Lead, Kindly Light, amid th' encircling
    gloom,
  Lead thou me on!
The night is dark, and I am far from
    home;
  Lead thou me on!
Keep thou my feet; I do not ask to see
The distant scene; one step enough for
    me.

I was not ever thus, nor prayed that
    thou
  Shouldst lead me on;
I loved to choose and see my path; but
    now
  Lead thou me on!
I loved the garish day, and, spite of
    fears,
Pride ruled my will. Remember not past
    years!

So long thy power hath blest me, sure
    it still
  Will lead me on
O'er moor and fen, o'er crag and
    torrent, till

The night is gone,
And with the morn those angel faces
    smile,
Which I have loved long since, and lost
    awhile.

           John Henry Newman

Lights

When we come home at night and
        close the door,
    Standing together in the shadowy
        room,
    Safe in our own love and the gentle
        gloom,
Glad of familiar wall and chair and floor,

Glad to leave far below the clanging
        city;
    Looking far downward to the glaring
        street
    Gaudy with light, yet tired with many
        feet
In both of us wells up a wordless pity;

Men have tried hard to put away the
        dark;
    A million lighted windows brilliantly
        Inlay with squares of gold the
        winter night,

But to us standing here there comes the stark
    Sense of the lives behind each yellow light,
And not one wholly joyous, proud or free.

                        Sara Teasdale

When I am tired of the road and of the endless parade of strange faces and alien places, I turn to Whitman. I see then that I am not to give in.

To a Stranger

Passing stranger! you do not know how
    longingly I look upon
  you,
You must be he I was seeking, or she I
    was seeking, (it comes
  to me as of a dream,)
I have somewhere surely lived a life of
    joy with you,
All is recall'd as we flit by each other,
    fluid, affectionate,
  chaste, matured,
You grew up with me, were a boy with
    me or a girl with me,
I ate with you and slept with you, your
    body has become not
  yours only nor left my body mine
  only,

You give me the pleasure of your eyes,
    face, flesh, as we
  pass, you take of my beard, breast,
    hands, in return,
I am not to speak to you, I am to think
    of you when I sit
  alone or wake at night alone,
I am to wait, I do not doubt I am to
    meet you again,
I am to see to it that I do not lose you.

Walt Whitman

I stood at Corinth, on the very podium where St. Paul is said to have spoken these words, and made my own recital of them to an audience who spoke no English. It has become one of my most moving performances.

❧

Though I speak with the tongues of
     men and of angels, and
have not charity, I am become as
     sounding brass, or a tinkling
cymbal.

And though I have the gift of prophecy,
     and understand all
mysteries, and all knowledge; and
     though I have all faith, so
that I could remove mountains, and
     have not charity, I am
nothing.

And though I bestow all my goods to
     feed the poor, and
though I give my body to be burned,
     and have not charity, it
profiteth me nothing.

Charity suffereth long, and is kind;
   charity envieth not; charity
vaunteth not itself, is not puffed up,

Doth not behave itself unseemly,
   seeketh not her own, is not
easily provoked, thinketh no evil;

Rejoiceth not in iniquity, but rejoiceth in
   the truth;

Beareth all things, believeth all things,
   hopeth all things,
endureth all things.

Charity never faileth: but whether there
   be prophecies, they
shall fail; whether there be tongues,
   they shall cease; whether
there be knowledge, it shall vanish
   away.

For we know in part, and we prophesy
   in part.

But when that which is perfect is come,
   then that which is in
part shall be done away.

When I was a child, I spake as a child, I
    understood as a
child, I thought as a child: but when I
    became a man, I put
away childish things.

For now we see through a glass, darkly;
    but then face to face:
now I know in part; but then shall I
    know even as also I am
known.

And now abideth faith, hope, charity,
    these three; but the
greatest of these is charity.

1 Corinthians 13

Stanzas Written on the Road Between Florence and Pisa

Oh, talk not to me of a name great in
　　story;
The days of our youth are the days of
　　our glory;
And the myrtle and ivy of sweet two-
　　and-twenty
Are worth all your laurels, though ever
　　so plenty.

What are garlands and crowns to the
　　brow that is wrinkled?
'Tis but as a dead flower with May-dew
　　besprinkled.
Then away with all such from the head
　　that is hoary!
What care I for the wreaths that can
　　only give glory?

O FAME!—if I e'er took delight in thy
　　praises,
'Twas less for the sake of thy high-
　　sounding phrases,
Than to see the bright eyes of the dear
　　one discover,

She thought that I was not unworthy to
    love her.

There chiefly I sought thee, there only I
    found thee;
Her glance was the best of the rays that
    surround thee;
When it sparkled o'er aught that was
    bright in my story,
I knew it was love, and I felt it was
    glory.

                         Lord Byron

The Character of a Happy Life

How happy is he born and taught
   That serveth not another's will;
Whose armour is his honest thought,
   And simple truth his utmost skill!

Whose passions not his masters are;
   Whose soul is still prepared for
     death,
Untied unto the world by care
   Of public fame or private breath;

Who envies none that chance doth
     raise;
   Nor vice hath ever understood
(How deepest wounds are given by
     praise!)
   Nor rules of State, but rules of good;

Who hath his life from rumours freed;
   Whose conscience is his strong
     retreat,
Whose state can neither flatterers feed,
   Nor ruin make oppressors great;

Who God doth late and early pray,
   More of his grace, than gifts, to lend,
And entertains the harmless day
   With a religious book or friend!

This man is freed from servile bands
   Of hope to rise or fear to fall!
Lord of himself, though not of lands;
   And having nothing, yet hath all!

Sir Henry Wotton

In All Things, Thanks!
THANKSGIVING AND PRAYER

When I was a little girl just starting out in the theater, I remember being suddenly disturbed one day about all the prayers going to God **asking** for something. I remember worrying that perhaps nobody ever thought about sending a prayer of thanks. So, one afternoon after rehearsal, I raced back to my room and, with the utmost care and concern, wrote out a prayer to God so full of thanksgiving that I was sure he would be overwhelmed. I knew that amidst the supplicant prayers he would be so grateful to receive this one thankful prayer that he would do something wonderful for the world.

I was probably still thinking the same thing the day the armistice was signed ending World War I. I was eighteen years old and in rehearsal on Broadway for **Dear Brutus.** Suddenly, a clamor arose in the street so loud that it could be heard in the theater. Somebody raced in and shouted the news that we had won. Chaos ensued! Nobody ever dismissed the cast, but everyone took off to drink and celebrate in the streets.

I, on the other hand, had nobler intentions. Racing out of the Empire Theatre, I headed straight to St. Patrick's Cathedral. All the while I had visions of being the only person in that vast chapel offering up a prayer of thanks to the Lord. But when I got there the cathedral was so packed I couldn't get inside! I was forced to offer my prayer from the steps.

I have lost the little prayer I wrote, and I have also lost some of the romanticism that pushed me, in part I'm sure, to St. Patrick's on that November day in 1918. But I have lost none of the sentiments with which I offered those heartfelt thanks. There is not a day that I look from my window here at Nyack on the Hudson that I do not remark on the shapes and the colors that gloriously surround my house. Not a day passes that I don't forget to whisper thanks. Most of my prayers, I am certain, are of thanksgiving. I still delight in finding a line or word that offers thanks in a new way.

I love to garden and I love to walk. These two things offer me ample opportunity to pray and to meditate on the passage of my days and the blessings I have known. I tend to shy away from talking about prayer, meditation, and religion. But that's not because I don't believe or don't pray. Really, it all comes so naturally.

When Charlie died I didn't run to church. But I didn't run to pills or alcohol either. I found peace and strength reading the Psalms. They were the same Psalms that had been on my bedside table for years and that I had read over and over again when my daughter died.

My friends also helped me adjust to Charlie's death. I was very confused, lonely, I guess. I even tried to sell our home and get away. But apparently God had other plans. Today I don't even feel lonely. I enjoy the solitude of my hillside walks and I revel in the pursuit of growing things. In both I see the handiwork of God. These are also the moments when I feel the closest to God.

I'm sure that everyone prays in the evening before sleep. I read often from my bedside prayer book the comforting words of the ages. But I also pray in my own words, sometimes even without using words at all. As I weed in the garden or stroll silently through the woods behind the house, I often enjoy a silent dialogue with God.

Of the two types of prayer—praying somebody else's words or praying my own—I cannot say which I think the best. While different, both are successful in what they hope to accomplish. The words of the poets and the prophets that I read at my bedside are melodious and splendid. My silent conversations with my God are fulfilling and fair.

It is perhaps more important now for me to rush to the Lord in thanksgiving than it was for me as a young girl in New York all those years ago. I have been truly blessed in my life. I have known much good and much love. I have also been given hard times, which I see, too, are in their own unique way a gift from God. Through the theater I have seen the most glorious and the most wretched paths the human soul can take. Through the glory of my home on the Hudson and the solitude of my home in Mexico, I have seen the most divine shapes God's creation can express. And I am thankful.

As part of my thanksgiving to God, I have brought forth this little book in the hope that someone may find the same inspiration and hope in the words that have aided me. If I help another through a dark time with my little anthology, it will be for me a means of thanking the One who provided for me. Read and find peace. Understand and find hope. Delve and enjoy!

The following few selections are some of my favorite prayers of thanksgiving.

God's World

O world, I cannot hold thee close
     enough!
     Thy winds, thy wide grey skies!
     Thy mists, that roll and rise!
Thy woods, this autumn day, that ache
     and sag
And all but cry with colour! That gaunt
     crag
To crush! To lift the lean of that black
     bluff!
World, World, I cannot get thee close
     enough!

Long have I known a glory in it all,
     But never knew I this:
     Here such a passion is
As stretcheth me apart,—Lord, I do
     fear

Thou'st made the world too beautiful
    this year;
My soul is all but out of me,—let fall
No burning leaf; prithee, let no bird call.

    Edna St. Vincent Millay

Prayer

God, though this life is but a wraith,
   Although we know not what we use,
Although we grope with little faith,
Give me the heart to fight—and lose.

Ever insurgent let me be,
   Make me more daring than devout;
From sleek contentment keep me free,
   And fill me with a buoyant doubt.

Open my eyes to visions girt
   With beauty, and with wonder lit—
But let me always see the dirt,
   And all that spawn and die in it.

Open my ears to music; let
   Me thrill with Spring's first flutes and
      drums—
But never let me dare forget
   The bitter ballads of the slums.

From compromise and things half-done,
   Keep me, with stern and stubborn
      pride;
And when, at last, the fight is won,
   God, keep me still unsatisfied.

Louis Untermeyer

Grace Before Sleep

How can our minds and bodies be
Grateful enough that we have spent
Here in this generous room, we three,
This evening of content?
Each one of us has walked through
    storm
And fled the wolves along the road;
But here the hearth is wide and warm,
And for this shelter and this light
Accept, O Lord, our thanks to-night.

                  Sara Teasdale

Watch, O Lord, with those who wake,
    or watch,
or weep tonight, and give your angels
    and saints
charge over those who sleep.
Tend your sick ones, O Lord Christ,
Rest your weary ones,
Bless your dying ones,

Soothe your suffering ones,
Pity your afflicted ones,
Shield your joyous ones,
And all for your love's sake.

St. Augustine

Awareness of God's Presence

O thou who are at home
Deep in my heart
Enable me to join you
Deep in my heart

The Talmud

Give us, Lord, a bit o' sun,
A bit o' work and a bit o' fun,
Give us in all the struggle and sputter,
Our daily bread and a bit o' butter,
Give us health our keep to make
And a bit to spare for other's sake
Give us, too, a bit of song,
And a tale and a book to help us along,
Give us, Lord, a chance to be
Our goodly best, brave, wise and free,
Our goodly best for ourselves and
    others
Till all men learn to live as brothers.

Old English

❈

May your heart be as patient
as the earth
Your love as warm as harvest gold.
May your days be full,
as the city is full
Your nights as joyful as dancers.
May your arms be as welcoming as
        home.
May your faith be as enduring
as God's love
Your spirit as valiant as your heritage.
May your hand be as sure as a friend
Your dreams as hopeful as a child.
May your soul be as brave as
your people.
And may you be blessed.

Roger Jan Radlowski
and John J. Kirvan

I thank you, Yahweh, with all my heart
because you have heard what I said.

The day I called for help, you heard me
and you increased my strength.

Psalm 138:1, 3

Thou hast given so much to me,
Give one thing more—a grateful heart:
Not thankful when it pleaseth me,
As if thy blessings had spare days,
But such a heart whose Pulse may be
Thy Praise.

George Herbert

Pied Beauty

Glory be to God for dappled things—
  For skies of couple-color as a brinded
    cow;
    For rose-moles all in stipple upon
    trout that swim;
Fresh-firecoal chestnut-falls; finches'
    wings;
  Landscape plotted and pieced—fold,
    fallow, and plough,
    And all trades, their gear and tackle
    and trim.

All things counter, original, spare,
    strange;
  Whatever is fickle, freckled (who
    knows how?)
    With swift, slow; sweet, sour;
    adazzle, dim;
He fathers-forth whose beauty is past
    change:
        Praise him.

Gerard Manley Hopkins

In my garden I find solitude. "No phones, no interruptions, I am busy," I say, then I go to my garden, shutting myself off there for a little while from the demands of daily living. Then I hear only the sounds of my garden, and what amusing, delightful, and fascinating sounds they are!

There is a family of mourning doves in one corner of the garden. They moan and moan—a soft, gentle sound—that always makes me think of springtime, of love being vocalized, of the Song of Solomon. Besides the mourning doves there are cardinals, whose songs are as brilliant as their plumage. There are also wild canaries in great numbers. And, while my birds provide me with a wonderful symphony, it is never distracting. I can think, dream, or, as I have done many, many times, learn the lines of a new play there.

The poet Thomas Edward Brown summed up the way I feel about my garden:

✤

A garden is a lovesome thing, God wot!
Rose plot, Fringed pool, Ferned grot—
  The veriest school
  Of peace; and yet the fool
Contends that God is not.
Not God! in gardens! when the eve is
    cool?
  Nay, but I have a sign:
  'Tis very sure God walks in mine.

Thomas Edward Brown

In my walks around the Hudson, in the growing things of my garden, in all things I find the beauty of God.

Loveliest of trees, the cherry now
Is hung with bloom along the bough,
And stands about the woodland ride
Wearing white for Eastertide.

Now, of my threescore years and ten,
Twenty will not come again,
And take from seventy springs a score,
It only leaves me fifty more.

And since to look at things in bloom
Fifty springs are little room,
About the woodlands I will go
To see the cherry hung with snow.

A. E. Housman

The Rhodora

In May, when sea-winds pierced our
    solitudes,
I found the fresh Rhodora in the woods,
Spreading its leafless blooms in a damp
    nook,
To please the desert and the sluggish
    brook.
The purple petals, fallen in the pool,
Made the black water with their beauty
    gay;
Here might the red-bird come his
    plumes to cool,
And court the flower that cheapens his
    array.
Rhodora! if the sages ask thee why
This charm is wasted on the earth and
    sky,
Tell them, dear, that if eyes were made
    for seeing,
Then Beauty is its own excuse for
    being:
Why thou wert there, O rival of the
    rose!

I never thought to ask, I never knew:
But, in my simple ignorance, suppose
The self-same Power that brought me
there brought you.

Ralph Waldo Emerson

Birches

When I see birches bend to left and
    right
Across the lines of straighter darker
    trees,
I like to think some boy's been
    swinging them.
But swinging doesn't bend them down
    to stay.
Ice-storms do that. Often you must
    have seen them
Loaded with ice a sunny winter morning
After a rain. They click upon
    themselves
As the breeze rises, and turn many-
    colored
As the stir cracks and crazes their
    enamel.
Soon the sun's warmth makes them
    shed crystal shells
Shattering and avalanching on the
    snow-crust—
Such heaps of broken glass to sweep
    away
You'd think the inner dome of heaven
    had fallen.

They are dragged to the withered
    bracken by the load,
And they seem not to break; though
    once they are bowed
So low for long, they never right
    themselves:
You may see their trunks arching in the
    woods
Years afterwards, trailing their leaves
    on the ground
Like girls on hands and knees that
    throw their hair
Before them over their heads to dry in
    the sun.
But I was going to say when Truth
    broke in
With all her matter-of-fact about the
    ice-storm
I should prefer to have some boy bend
    them
As he went out and in to fetch the
    cows—
Some boy too far from town to learn
    baseball,
Whose only play was what he found
    himself,

Summer or winter, and could play
　　alone.
One by one he subdued his father's
　　trees
By riding them down over and over
　　again
Until he took the stiffness out of them,
And not one but hung limp, not one
　　was left
For him to conquer. He learned all there
　　was
To learn about not launching out too
　　soon
And so not carrying the tree away
Clear to the ground. He always kept his
　　poise
To the top branches, climbing carefully
With the same pains you use to fill a
　　cup
Up to the brim, and even above the
　　brim.
Then he flung outward, feet first, with a
　　swish,
Kicking his way down through the air to
　　the ground.
So was I once myself a swinger of
　　birches.

And so I dream of going back to be.
It's when I'm weary of considerations,
And life is too much like a pathless
    wood
Where your face burns and tickles with
    the cobwebs
Broken across it, and one eye is
    weeping
From a twig's having lashed across it
    open.
I'd like to get away from earth awhile
And then come back to it and begin
    over.
May no fate willfully misunderstand me
And half grant what I wish and snatch
    me away
Not to return. Earth's the right place for
    love:
I don't know where it's likely to go
    better.
I'd like to go by climbing a birch tree,
And climb black branches up a snow-
    white trunk
Toward heaven, till the tree could bear
    no more,
But dipped its top and set me down
    again.

That would be good both going and
     coming back.
One could do worse than be a swinger
     of birches.

              Robert Frost

Here are two popular music lyrics which I find quite lovely.

Sunshine on My Shoulders

Sunshine on my shoulders makes me
    happy,
Sunshine in my eyes can make me cry.
Sunshine on the water looks so lovely,
Sunshine almost always makes me
    high.

If I had a day that I could give you,
I'd give to you a day just like today.
If I had a song that I could sing for you,
I'd sing a song to make you feel this
    way.

Sunshine on my shoulders makes me
    happy,
Sunshine in my eyes can make me cry.
Sunshine on the water looks so lovely,
Sunshine almost always makes me
    high.

If I had a tale that I could tell you,
I'd tell a tale sure to make you smile.
If I had a wish that I could wish for you,
I'd make a wish for sunshine all the
while.

John Denver

Day by Day

Day by day, day by day
Oh, dear Lord, three things I Pray:
To see thee more clearly,
Love thee more dearly,
Follow thee more nearly
Day by day.

> Richard of Chichester,
> thirteenth century,
> as quoted in the
> musical "Godspell"

Where Is Heaven?

Where is Heaven? Is it not
Just a friendly garden plot,
Walled with stone and roofed with sun,
Where the days pass one by one
Not too fast and not too slow,
Looking backward as they go
At the beauties left behind
To transport the pensive mind.

Does not Heaven begin that day
When the eager heart can say,
Surely God is in this place,
I have seen Him face to face
In the loveliness of flowers,
In the service of the showers,
And His voice has talked to me
In the sunlit apple tree.

Bliss Carman

The Most Steadfast of Lines

In this section are some of the most revered words I know. The pages in my books that contain these selections are dogeared and soiled from the countless times in my life when I have turned to them for comfort and consolation. They are the oldest and the dearest of my friends, the most faithful and the most firm.

The following few selections have probably done more for humanity than countless tomes on library shelves. I would be foolish and indeed a bit careless to write a book of this sort and leave them out. If the other lines in my little book are jewels, then these are certainly the crown jewels.

I will lift up mine eyes unto the hills,
    from whence cometh
my help.

My help cometh from the Lord, which
    made heaven and
earth.

He will not suffer thy foot to be moved:
    he that keepeth thee
will not slumber.

Behold, he that keepeth Israel shall
    neither slumber nor sleep.

The Lord is thy keeper: the Lord is thy
    shade upon thy right
hand.

The sun shall not smite thee by day, nor
    the moon by night.

The Lord shall preserve thee from all
    evil: he shall preserve
thy soul.

The Lord shall preserve thy going out
    and thy coming in from
this time forth, and even for evermore.

Psalm 121

Bless the Lord, O my soul: and all that
    is within me, bless his
holy name.

Bless the Lord, O my soul, and forget
    not all his benefits:

Who forgiveth all thine iniquities; who
    healeth all thy
diseases;

Who redeemeth thy life from
    destruction; who crowneth thee
with lovingkindness and tender
    mercies;

Who satisfieth thy mouth with good
    things; so that thy youth
is renewed like the eagle's.

134

The Lord executeth righteousness and
    judgment for all that
are oppressed.

He made known his ways unto Moses,
    his acts unto the
children of Israel.

The Lord is merciful and gracious, slow
    to anger, and
plenteous in mercy.

Psalm 103:1-8

❀

The Lord is my shepherd; I shall not
  want.

He maketh me to lie down in green
    pastures: he leadeth me
beside the still waters.

He restoreth my soul: he leadeth me in
    the paths of
righteousness for his name's sake.

Yea, though I walk through the valley of
    the shadow of
death, I will fear no evil: for thou art
    with me; thy rod and
thy staff they comfort me.

Thou preparest a table before me in the
    presence of
mine enemies: thou anointest my head
    with oil; my cup
runneth over.

Surely goodness and mercy shall follow
    me all the days of
my life: and I will dwell in the house of
    the Lord for ever.

Psalm 23

Make a joyful noise unto the Lord, all ye
lands.

Serve the Lord with gladness: come
before his presence with
singing.

Know ye that the Lord he is God: it is
he that hath made us,
and not we ourselves; we are his
people, and the sheep of his
pasture.

Enter into his gates with thanksgiving,
and into his courts with
praise: be thankful unto him, and bless
his name.

For the Lord is good; his mercy is
everlasting; and his truth
endureth to all generations.

Psalm 100

✣

In the beginning God created the
heavens and the earth.
The earth was without form and void,
and darkness was upon
the face of the deep; and the Spirit of
God was moving over
the face of the waters.

And God said, ''Let there be light''; and
there was light. And
God saw that the light was good.

And God saw everything that he had
made, and behold, it
was very good.

Genesis 1:1-4, 31

For God so loved the world, that he
    gave his only begotten
Son, that whosoever believeth in him
    should not perish,
but have everlasting life.

John 3:16

God grant me the serenity to accept.
    things I cannot change,
courage to change things I can, and
    wisdom to know the
difference.

St. Teresa of Avila

Desiderata

Go placidly amid the noise & haste, &
      remember what peace
there may be in silence. As far as
      possible without surrender,
be on good terms with all persons.
      Speak your truth quietly &
clearly; and listen to others, even the
      dull & ignorant; they,
too, have their story. ☆ Avoid loud &
      aggressive persons, they
are vexations to the spirit. If you
      compare yourself with
others, you may become vain & bitter;
      for always there will
be greater & lesser persons than
      yourself. Enjoy your
achievements as well as your plans. ☆
      Keep interested in
your own career, however humble; it is
      a real possession in
the changing fortunes of time. Exercise
      caution in your
business affairs; for the world is full of
      trickery. But let this

not blind you to what virtue there is;
     many persons strive for
high ideals; and everywhere life is full of
     heroism. ☆ Be
yourself. Especially, do not feign
     affection. Neither be cynical
about love; for in the face of all aridity
     & disenchantment it is
perennial as the grass. ☆ Take kindly
     the counsel of the
years, gracefully surrendering the things
     of youth. Nurture
strength of spirit to shield you in
     sudden misfortune. But do
not distress yourself with imaginings.
     Many fears are born of
fatigue & loneliness. Beyond a
     wholesome discipline, be
gentle with yourself. ☆ You are a child
     of the universe, no
less than the trees & the stars; you
     have a right to be here.
And whether or not it is clear to you,
     no doubt the universe is
unfolding as it should. ☆ Therefore be
     at peace with God,

141

whatever you conceive Him to be, and
        whatever your labors
& aspirations, in the noisy confusion of
        life keep peace with
your soul. ☆ With all its sham,
        drudgery & broken dreams, it
is still a beautiful world. Be cheerful.
        Strive to be happy.

Max Ehrmann

If

If you can keep your head when all
    about you
  Are losing theirs and blaming it on
    you;
If you can trust yourself when all men
    doubt you,
  But make allowance for their doubting
    too:
If you can wait and not be tired by
    waiting,
  Or, being lied about, don't deal in
    lies,
Or being hated don't give way to
    hating,
  And yet don't look too good, nor talk
    too wise;

If you can dream—and not make
    dreams your master;
  If you can think—and not make
    thoughts your aim,
If you can meet with Triumph and
    Disaster
  And treat those two impostors just
    the same:

If you can bear to hear the truth you've
spoken
Twisted by knaves to make a trap for
fools,
Or watch the things you gave your life
to, broken,
And stoop and build 'em up with
worn-out tools;

If you can make one heap of all your
winnings
And risk it on one turn of pitch-and-
toss,
And lose, and start again at your
beginnings,
And never breathe a word about your
loss:
If you can force your heart and nerve
and sinew
To serve your turn long after they are
gone,
And so hold on when there is nothing in
you
Except the Will which says to them:
"Hold on!"

If you can talk with crowds and keep
your virtue,

Or walk with Kings—nor lose the
common touch,
If neither foes nor loving friends can
hurt you,
If all men count with you, but none
too much:
If you can fill the unforgiving minute
With sixty seconds' worth of
distance run,
Yours is the Earth and everything that's
in it,
And—which is more—you'll be a
Man, my son!

Rudyard Kipling

This, then, is how you should pray:
"Our Father in heaven:
May your holy name be honored;
may your Kingdom come;
may your will be done on earth as it
   is in heaven.
Give us today the food we need.
Forgive us the wrongs we have done,
   as we forgive the wrongs that
   others have done to us.
Do not bring us to hard testing,
   but keep us safe from the Evil
   One."

Matthew 6:9-13

The Beatitudes

''Blessed are the poor in spirit,
   for theirs is the kingdom of heaven.
''Blessed are they who mourn,
   for they shall be comforted.
''Blessed are the meek,
   for they shall possess the earth.
''Blessed are they who hunger and
      thirst for justice,
   for they shall have their fill.
''Blessed are the merciful,
   for they shall obtain mercy.
''Blessed are the clean of heart,
   for they shall see God.
''Blessed are the peacemakers,
   for they shall be called the children of
      God.
''Blessed are they who suffer
      persecution for justice's sake,
   for theirs is the kingdom of heaven.''

Adapted from Matthew 5:3-10

For everything there is a season,
and a time for every matter under
heaven:
a time to be born, and a time to die;
a time to plant, and a time to pluck up
what is planted;
a time to kill, and a time to heal;
a time to break down, and a time to
build up;
a time to weep, and a time to laugh;
a time to mourn, and a time to dance;
a time to cast away stones, and a time
to gather stones together;
a time to embrace, and a time to refrain
from embracing;
a time to seek, and a time to lose;
a time to keep, and a time to cast
away;
a time to rend, and a time to sew;
a time to keep silence, and a time to
speak;
a time to love, and a time to hate;
a time for war, and a time for peace.
What gain has the worker from his toil?

Ecclesiastes 3:1-9

Finally, my most favorite poem of all times. Of all the glorious lines ever written, I cherish these the most:

Great fleas have little fleas upon their
   backs to bite 'em,
And little fleas have lesser fleas, and so
   ad infinitum.

Augustus De Morgan

<u>Acknowledgments</u>

The author has made every reasonable attempt to acquire and secure permissions for all materials quoted or otherwise used in this work. Any sources not adequately or accurately cited will be corrected in future editions.

"Annie's Song." Words and music by John Denver. Copyright © 1974—Cherry Lane Music Publishing Co., Inc. All rights reserved. Used by permission.

"Birches," "Devotion," and "Reluctance." From **The Poetry of Robert Frost,** edited by Edward Connery Lathem. Copyright 1916, 1934, 1928 © 1969 by Holt, Rinehart and Winston. Copyright 1944 © 1956, 1962 by Robert Frost. Reprinted by permission of Holt, Rinehart and Winston, Publishers.

Large Print Inspirational Books
from
Walker

Would you like to be on our
Large Print mailing list?

Please send your
name and address to:

Beth Walker
Walker and Company
720 Fifth Avenue
New York, NY 10019

Among the titles available are:

The Road Less Traveled
M. Scott Peck, M.D.

Words to Love By
Mother Teresa

**Three Steps Forward,
Two Steps Back**
Charles R. Swindoll

Getting Through the Night
Eugenia Price

Surprised by Joy
C. S. Lewis

Hinds' Feet on High Places
Hannah Hurnard

Hope and Faith for Tough Times
Robert H. Schuller

Irregular People
Joyce Landorf

**The Little Flowers of
St. Francis of Assisi**

Prayers and Promises for Every Day
Corrie ten Boom

Out of Solitude
Henri J.M. Nouwen

God at Eventide
A.J. Russell

Glorious Intruder
Joni Eareckson Tada

Your God Is Too Small
J.B. Phillips

Peace, Love and Healing
Bernie Siegel

The Secret Kingdom
Pat Robertson

Sea Edge
W. Phillip Keller

Peace With God
Billy Graham

Opening to God
Thomas H. Green, S.J.

Not I, But Christ
Corrie ten Boom

Beyond Codependency
Melody Beattie

A Diary of Private Prayer
John Baillie

Beginning to Pray
Anthony Bloom

Gift from the Sea
Anne Morrow Lindbergh

Words to Love By
Mother Teresa

A Gathering of Hope
Helen Hayes

A Grief Observed
C.S. Lewis

Apples of Gold
Jo Petty

The Practice of the Presence of God
Brother Lawrence

Words of Certitude
Pope John Paul II

Codependent No More
Melody Beattie

The Power of Positive Thinking
Norman Vincent Peale

The True Joy of Positive Living
Norman Vincent Peale

Reflections on the Psalms
C.S. Lewis

The Genesee Diary
Henri J.M. Nouwen

Reaching Out
Henri J.M. Nouwen

To Help You Through the Hurting
Marjorie Holmes

With Open Hands
Henri J.M. Nouwen

Introducing the Bible
William Barclay

To God Be the Glory
Billy Graham & Corrie ten Boom

God in the Hard Times
Dale Evans Rogers

Surprised By Suffering
R.C. Sproul

He Began with Eve
Joyce Landorf

Insomnia
God's Night School
Connie Soth

Good Morning, Holy Spirit
Benny Hinn

Strength to Love
Martin Luther King, Jr.

The Burden Is Light
Eugenia Price